The Miscarriage Project

Testimonials of Parents Who Found Hope in God

AUTHOR

A.C. Babbitt

For more information, visit acbabbitt.com

or email acbabbitt_author@acbabbitt.com

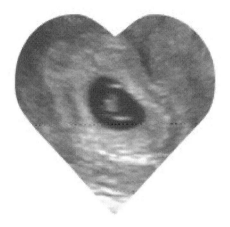

In memory of our son, Timothy Lyle Babbitt. You are always loved, always cherished, always remembered, forever in our hearts.

To parents around the world who've experienced miscarriage, this book is for you.

I pray you find hope in God and His Word, and the comfort and healing you are looking for.

Acknowledgments

I thank God, first and foremost, for His enduring faithfulness and compassion throughout my grief journey. Thank you for guiding me in the writing and publishing of this book. To Him be the glory forever and ever. Amen.

Thank you to those who contributed their testimonies to make this book possible.

I can't thank you enough for your willingness to share your sufferings for the healing of others. May God continue to bless you and your families!

Thank you to my family and friends for your continued prayers, support, and encouragement to keep going, to press on toward the goal, and finish *The Miscarriage Project*. I couldn't have done it without you!

PREFACE

You and I are in the same boat. If you're reading this now, chances are you've lost a child, as I have. Whether you have had a miscarriage, stillbirth, lost an infant after he or she was born, gave them up for adoption, or even aborted a baby, there's grace for you here.

My goal for this testimonial is to provide a tool for you that I wish I'd had as I trudged through the painful, grieving loss of my baby Timothy in the womb. My prayer for you is to find healing, but also to find God's love and mercy on your journey each day. It hasn't been an easy journey for me, but I can tell you my journey has taken me in many directions—most of which I didn't see coming.

Take this testimonial, for instance. I can't tell you how many times God has been asking me to write this for you, but I refused. I did everything I could to avoid it or make excuses not to write, because I was scared, but even more, I was angry. Angry that God didn't answer my prayers to save our son. Angry because I felt God had broken His promises to me—promises to protect me and that His plans were for my good—prosperous, hopeful plans. Every time I tried to read Scripture, instead of finding comfort and peace, it just fueled my raging fire.

Eventually, though, I began to write a blog. This blog documents my journey through grief as it was happening. God pressed on my heart that this blog was to be free, to reach those suffering women who wouldn't purchase or couldn't afford to purchase a book. I kid you not. Women (and maybe men too) around the world have read my story, and my only hope is that they found comfort, healing, and an enduring faith in Jesus Christ.

As you read this book of testimonials rooted in Scripture and based on my personal experience, most of which came from my first blog, as well as various parents' stories I have included, I pray you find the comfort and healing you are looking for. You're not alone in your suffering. I'm amazed how many women have suffered in silence and, even more painfully, faced a society that doesn't acknowledge a fetus lost as a loved and valuable child. Let God do a work in you that will change your life. Let God redeem and restore what you've lost. He loves you and cares for you so much more than you could even imagine. Let's walk this journey together—let's go!

A.C. Babbitt
Timothy's Mom

GET FREE
3-IN-1 RESOURCE

WHEN YOU VISIT THE LINK BELOW,
YOU CAN DOWNLOAD THIS FREE 3-IN-1 MISCARRIAGE
RESOURCE FOR FREE!

INCLUDES "WHAT TO SAY & WHAT NOT TO SAY", "EMOTIONAL
HEALTH CHECK-UP" AND "ASK YOUR DOCTOR" PROMPTS.

ACBABBITT.COM

MISCARRIAGE
RESOURCES

3 IN 1 GUIDE FOR PARENTS & SUPPORTERS
AFTER MISCARRIAGE

ACBABBITT.COM

AC
BABBITT

LINK:
HTTPS://WWW.SUBSCRIBEPAGE.COM
/THEMISCARRIAGEPROJECT

TABLE OF CONTENTS

CHAPTER 1

THE MISCARRIAGE

May 26, 2016

I hadn't felt like myself for that month leading up to the miscarriage. I thought it was because of a small fight I'd had with a family member that I just couldn't seem to overcome, but it turns out my body was already grieving the loss of my unborn child.

At MOPS, two days before the bleeding started, I hugged a friend who had just shared she was wrestling with God because she'd experienced her second miscarriage two and a half weeks earlier. When I hugged her, I felt such a connection with her, and I sobbed with her. I couldn't figure out at the time why I was crying so hard. Now I know God was preparing for me a friend who knew only too well what I'm experiencing now.

Two weeks ago, on Monday, May 9, 2016, we lost our precious Timothy Lyle Babbitt. He was nine weeks and six days old in the womb. According to the doctor, he most likely had been gone for a month already, because by the ultrasound, Timothy only measured five weeks and six days old. So I don't really know how to age him for sure. I can't fully express the deep, dark despair of knowing I'd carried my dead, unborn child for a month and had no idea. It was as if my womb had become a tomb—a place of death instead of life.

I'm the mom; I should have known! I should have protected him or something, but now I'm powerless to do anything but imagine him. I hate the word *miscarriage*, as if I made a mistake carrying my baby or wasn't suitable somehow. It's the loss of a child, not simply bloody tissue your body disposes of once it has figured out *it* is not alive anymore.

My prayer to God wasn't answered, at least not in the way I'd hoped. I know God will use it for good, and in God's goodness, He allowed me to see and hear my son in a dream. Timothy looked like my oldest son, who is two years old now, and was dressed in a white T-shirt and shorts. Standing in front of me in a bright light, among the green grass, he smiled at me and said in that sweet child voice, "Hi, Mommy! I made it. I'm okay. I love you!"

God knew how to comfort me. He gave enough to sustain me, in my ever-mourning heart, and that was to see my son, my Timothy, *my little love.*

CHAPTER 2

THE WORST MOTHER'S DAY OF MY LIFE

May 30, 2016

I didn't see it coming. I had all the signs and symptoms, but I had no idea what to look for. I wasn't supposed to have a miscarriage. Not me. I'd had two beautiful, healthy children before this. Why would I have a miscarriage now? I was dead wrong.

I'd been experiencing cramps, sharp pains, and lightheadedness that week. However, I hadn't noticed these as bad signs or worrisome symptoms. Nonetheless, starting that Saturday morning, I began to bleed, something like a light period. The bleeding didn't stop but got heavier, so we went into the ER that evening. The nurses and the doctor on call were trying to give us a shred of hope to hold on to, but they also were preparing us for the worst. They said it could be normal bleeding during the pregnancy or I could be in the early stages of miscarriage.

That Sunday just happened to be Mother's Day, and I couldn't breathe. I couldn't bear to celebrate, not knowing whether I was losing my child or not. We'd had the ultrasound, and the baby had looked fine, but there was no heartbeat, so I wasn't so sure we had a chance Timothy would still be alive. We sobbed and sobbed and sobbed some more, grieving so deeply before we even knew for sure.

On Monday morning, I woke up around three forty-five in the blood of my womb. I knew then that my baby was really gone. There was no hope left to hold, no child to care for. My baby Timothy, the child I never held in my arms, was gone. The worst day of my life!

I'm thankful I had the privilege to carry him in my womb the short time I did, but it seems like the blink of an eye now. Gone, unseen, not forgotten, but not acknowledged by anyone who never knew our third child. Since when do numbers matter? Since people think I only have two children, but I had three. The third lives in heaven, not with me or his family. Timothy lives, as does my love for him as his mom.

CHAPTER 3

WAS IT MY FAULT?

June 1, 2016

There's not a day that goes by that I don't wonder if there was something else, I could have done to save my baby. I wish it didn't feel like my fault, like there was something I could have done to change the outcome of what happened. I could have done something, right?

But I didn't. There were some things I possibly could have done differently, but I'll never know for sure. I didn't realize by not changing those few little things, I wasn't choosing Timothy. I wasn't choosing my son. And that is my biggest regret of all. I was so afraid, nervous, and overwhelmed, and now I just want my baby back.

After writing this first part in my journal, I read Deuteronomy 28, which talks about the blessings for obeying God and the curses for disobeying God. The following writing includes the verses and my conclusion after reading them:

And if you faithfully obey the voice of the Lord your God, being careful to do all his commandments that I command you today, the Lord your God will set you high above all the nations of the earth. And all these blessings shall

come upon you and overtake you, if you obey the voice of the Lord your God. … Blessed shall be the fruit of your womb and the fruit of your ground and the fruit of your cattle, the increase of your herds and the young of your flock. … But if you will not obey the voice of the Lord your God or be careful to do all his commandments and his statutes that I command you today, then all these curses shall come upon you and overtake you. … Cursed shall be the fruit of your womb and the fruit of your ground, the increase of your herds and the young of your flock. (Deuteronomy 28:1–2, 4, 15, 18 ESV)

After reading this, I know "cursed is the fruit of your womb" doesn't apply to us, because we do follow God and obey Him the best we can. Better yet, how can a baby be cursed if it's in heaven? I feel more peace of mind, but I know we have a long journey ahead of us. I just hope my husband and I are together even through this trial. I really hope so. We have amazing support where we are. I hope it's enough.

* * * * *

Last week, during Pastor's Conference at Moody Bible Institute, our alma mater, we attended a workshop led by Jesse Campbell. He talked about his twin son, Aiden, whom they had lost, and how many people came to know Jesus through their constant faith in the midst of pain and tragedy. He also talked about how bad things happen for three reasons:

1. They are a result of sin, as in the story of King David and Bathsheba (2 Samuel 11).
2. Satan is wreaking havoc on your life just as he did to Job (Job 1).
3. They are happening for God's glory, as in the story of the man born blind (John 9).

I realized then that it couldn't have been our fault. We didn't lose Timothy because we had sinned but because Satan had wreaked havoc on our lives and because our loss would ultimately give God glory. Knowing I didn't hurt my son gives me peace and comfort.

Though God has taken away the most precious thing He ever could, Timothy is safe in the arms of Jesus, and I couldn't ask for a better person to raise him. I even prayed for God to help me to look forward to heaven and eternal life more, and He has. I so hope to spend eternity with Timothy and not to miss more of his life than I have to.

CHAPTER 4

THE TALE OF A CHICAGO FRIEND

June 3, 2016

Since starting my blog and documenting my grief journey, several women have shared their tragic miscarriage, stillborn, or infant loss stories with me. This testimony is from one such woman, a friend from our Chicago days. With her permission, I share and summarize her story.

May 26, 2016

Thank you for sharing about the loss of your child. Just wanted to let you know that we know what you're going through, I guess. We, too, lost a child last month. It was early as well (maybe four to five weeks), but I started bleeding on April 26, and then it was about four to five days. April 26 just happened to be my first OB appointment—with a new OB too. Because I was bleeding and my cervix was open, they didn't want to do an ultrasound. I could have pushed for it, but I think I was so in shock that I just did the HCG blood test and left.

We prayed that God would let us keep our child, that I was bleeding for some other reason, but it wasn't His plan. I think going through the physical part was the hardest for me, knowing that my body was, in a way, giving birth, but to a child that was in heaven already. I cried so much, but at the same time, I was numb. So many emotions just rushing through me, not to mention the horrible hormonal stuff. Uncharted territory that I just went through like a robot, not knowing what to expect each day. I just prayed for God to be with me every step of the way and He was.

Your dream is such a cool thing. God is *so* good! We didn't know if our child was a boy or girl, but I think it was a girl. I keep thinking girl, and "girl" comes out when I talk about our child (baby {last name}). I guess I won't know for sure until heaven. God has given me such comfort and peace, even though I've been a total wreck emotionally. Just tonight, when I was doing our prayer with our son (my husband is gone until tomorrow), I was ending, and he asked to pray for baby. We used to pray for the baby, with him, before we knew of our loss. Anyway, it was the sweetest thing. So, we prayed as tears just rolled down my cheeks as they are now. Such a gift to me tonight. Then I read your story.

We will be praying for your comfort. I'm so very sorry.

* * * * *

June 3, 2016

This is what I read in my devotion today. "Blessed be the God and Father of our Lord Jesus Christ, the Father of mercies and God of all comfort, who comforts us in all our affliction, so that we may be able to comfort those who are in any affliction, with the comfort with which we ourselves are comforted by God. For as we share abundantly in Christ's sufferings, so through Christ we share abundantly in comfort too" (2 Corinthians 1:3–5 ESV).[1]

This was so encouraging to me, so wanted to pass it on. I also wanted to share something my husband said that is really helping me when I get the emotions flowing. I told him I just wanted to curl up in a ball in my bed and never get up. He said that he needed me, and our son needed me.

This was early on, but it's really helped me stand strong when the sadness pulls me in. So maybe that will help you? Chuck needs you as well as your two beautiful little children. Our babies are in the best hands we could possibly dream, and though it hurts deep here on earth, we can definitely trust God to take care of our babies.

Someday I'll probably write about it too, but

I know sharing is very powerful so share away. Continuing to pray for you guys!

Anonymous Mom

My dear friend expressed much of the same feelings I'd been [1] feeling, during the early weeks following the miscarriage. So, I wanted to share her encouragements as well. Don't hesitate to share your story. It's more healing than you can imagine.

---

[11] The Holy Bible, English Standard Version. ESV Text Edition: 2016. Copyright © 2001 by Crossway Bibles, a publishing ministry of Good News Publishers.

CHAPTER 5

EVERY CHILD COUNTS!

May 26, 2016

Today was an amazing day! God had me start a blog today entitled *The Child I Never Held*. People are already being impacted and are responding to our story about losing Timothy. We are even feeling led to share our story when we reconnect with old college classmates, and even complete strangers, here at Moody's Pastors' Conference.

My husband thinks I talk to too many people sometimes (which he does too), but I felt led to stop and wait to talk to Aaron Shust's wife, Sarah, after his concert tonight at Pastor's Conference (Moody Bible Institute, Chicago, Illinois). We talked about our kids and how I valued her supporting Aaron by attending his concert. They have three sons, but she talked about one in particular, Michael. Michael is four years old, but looks like he is one year old, she said, because he has half a heart and has Down syndrome. I love the family pictures she showed me, so happy and so much love there!

She genuinely cared to hear about Timothy, losing him, and   so on. I felt like I'd been graciously counseled afterward because she affirmed for me, "No, you have three (children), and Jesus is holding one of them." I thanked her for giving me permission to acknowledge to people that we not only have the two visible kids, but our third child is in Heaven—and always counts. Every child counts!

She was so kind, sweet, genuinely cared and listened— not a "roadie" wife that only cares about fame and not people. No, she was one of the most genuine, loving people I have ever met. Praise God for orchestrating that encounter with her. Thank you, God,   for that confirmation and permission to count *all* three of my children, and to meet such a compassionate person.

Even the words of the songs Aaron shared tonight— some new, old, and current— really resonated with me. One song about fear was especially touching, a new song called "Fear Not." This song reminded me not to be afraid because God is with me. I don't have to face life alone. I don't have to face grief alone either. God is opening so many doors—it's an exciting time. Let us not forget your goodness and truth, Lord Jesus. *Amen.*

CHAPTER 6

THE MILESTONE HE NEVER REACHED

May 31, 2016

Today, I had another hCG hormone blood test done again to see if my hormone levels have returned to zero after the miscarriage. I haven't heard the results yet, but I'm nervous. If it's zero, I won't be pregnant (again, as I'd hoped), but if it's higher than last time, then our journey with number four begins all over again. I'm afraid to be in constant fear for nine to ten months, and what that could do to our family and our marriage. I don't want to be the one marked as the "one who had the miscarriage," I want to be the "one who is having a baby" again—like I was before.

I saw a friend of ours, as I was leaving the doctor's office, and she had her six-day-old son with her—what a sweetheart! But then it hit me. The pang of longing that will never be satisfied, or so it would seem. The longing to hold my baby boy, my sweet child, my Timothy. Timothy would've been thirteen weeks along today, making it even more painful.

I tricked myself into believing that once our friend (and others) had their baby, it would be easier to be in their company. I wish I hadn't been wrong. The grief seems to drown me all over again, and I couldn't help but cry for my loss and the empty longing I'm left to hold and keep.

My husband was so kind and held me close so I wouldn't feel so sad or alone. I'm so blessed he has been so steady in this time of chaos and confusion—yet there is still love and peace among us. I can't tell you how wonderfully amazing it is to have married the man God chose for me, my love for life, my best friend.

Truly, God does know the best love for me and how best to love and comfort me; truly, He does.

CHAPTER 7

THE AUTHENTICITY OF A GRIEVING MOM

June 20, 2019

This testimony is the raw, authentic, yet beautiful testimony of a mom who was so angry with God, following her miscarriage. With her permission, this is her story:

I have two kids. Two happy, healthy, beautiful kids. They make me happy beyond belief and I'm so proud to be their mom! I have also had one loss—one sad, depressing loss. My miscarriage happened between the births of my two children and was one of the hardest things I've ever had to go through. If you met me today, you'd never know how sad I used to be. Let me tell you a little bit about my story.

My husband and I were married for two years before we decided to start trying to have children. We had our fun "us" time, and once we were ready to start having children, I thought it wouldn't take long. *Wrong.* We tried for over a year and a half to have our first. Between his busy schedule, my stress of wanting to get pregnant, and our timing, it was hard. I started praying to God. I prayed to Him to help bless us with a beautiful baby. And He did. Before I became pregnant, I prayed to Him for a healthy pregnancy. I said to Him, "Please don't let me become pregnant if it's not meant to be. I could never suffer a loss." My prayers were answered, and I was beyond blessed with a healthy baby boy!

Fast-forward two years later. We were ready to try for our second, and, boy, did we try! It took almost a year for us to get pregnant again, but we did. Again, I prayed to God for a healthy pregnancy. By now, I thought He knew that I couldn't handle a loss. I have a history of anxiety and depression, and to lose a child would just be too much for me to handle. He knew that right? He wouldn't put me through that. But He did.

I was twelve weeks pregnant when I found out I'd miscarried. After an ultrasound, the baby measured in at seven weeks. Ummm … that's a five week difference! I had zero signs that I'd miscarried. No cramps, no spotting, no nothing. I was sad; so sad. And, boy, was I mad. I was mad at God. This was His fault. I'd prayed to Him over and over and over for a healthy pregnancy, and He didn't give me that. I let him know that I couldn't handle a loss like that, and I only wanted to be pregnant if it was really meant to be. Why did He allow this to happen? Why would He put me through this? I cussed at

Him; I cursed His name. I even yelled out loud at Him. I felt my faith start to fade.

After I had some time to heal (and be mad at God, because let's be real—I felt like I had every right to be mad at Him because after all, this was *His* fault!), I started talking to Him again. I figured

I'd taken enough time "off" and it was now time to question Him and process what happened. My little seven-week-old baby was not meant to be. Maybe it wouldn't have been born healthy. Maybe complications during pregnancy would've occurred. Maybe something would've happened to me. No matter what the future would've brought, this little babe was not meant to be in it. It took some time for me to get back on track with my relationship with God, but it happened. I allowed myself time to sulk, be upset, and be mad at Him and I'm glad I did. It helped strengthen my relationship with Him, and both the big man and I are in a better place.

After a few months, I was ready to try again for another baby. My husband was also on board with this, as we have always talked about wanting two children, and let's be honest, what man doesn't enjoy the baby making process?

It took several months before I was pregnant again, and after my initial bout of excitement came fear. What if He was going to allow me to have another loss? What if this baby wasn't meant to come into our world? The first twelve weeks were the scariest, but once I made it through that (with a little faith involved), it was smooth sailing. Several months later, we were blessed with a beautiful baby girl. I was over-the-moon ecstatic, and my dream for a family of four had become a reality. I was thankful and overjoyed.

I might have blamed God for my miscarriage, but I also give Him credit for my two amazing and happy children. My relationship with Him grew, and today, I am in a happy place.

If you experience a loss, allow yourself time to grieve and time to be mad. As I sit here today and type this up, I can't help but sit and stare at my beautiful children that I thank God for every single day.

Melissa P.

CHAPTER 8

TALKING TO GOD

June 4, 2016

My firstborn son (age two) jumped hard into my lap unexpectedly today during playtime. It hurt so bad I burst into tears! I left the room, which my son felt bad about, but I think I really needed the space to cry out to God.

"Why did God take my baby? He was my son! Where's my baby?" I cry out to God over and over. Where my two-year-old old fell on me is where Timothy used to be. "Where's my baby? Why couldn't I keep him with me?" I sobbed until I couldn't sob anymore. I could tell I just needed a good cry.

Then I asked God those questions again, but actually took the time to listen for His answers. God said Timothy was never mine, always His. Then I asked why I carried him in the first place, and I realized every child needs a mama. They have Him as their Heavenly Father - but every child needs a mama. Some things God says aren't super clear at first, but become clearer over time. I hope that is true with the miscarriage too.

I also have to remember that God has numbered our days, and Timothy's days were just shorter than most. God reassured me this was always part of the plan, to help others, but it's still painful beyond belief! I have lost my third child, my second son—but

I have gained hope in knowing he's the safest he could be, the happiest he could be, and in the best place he could be. I just hope someday that will be enough reassurance to be fully comforted. The void still aches, the sadness is still drowning, the heartache still stings— but love ever hopes. Love endures. Love perseveres. Love never ends (1 Corinthians 13).

P.S. I pray we never miscarry ever again, and I pray our next child will come at just the right time—in enough time to grieve, but not too long, I hope. I never know when my husband will be ready, but I trust God will make him ready.

CHAPTER 9

THE BEWILDERED PASTOR

June 1, 2019

This testimony is written by my husband, Timothy's father. This is his struggle, to be supportive of me, but he was trying to process his own grief at the same time. With his permission, this is his story:

I'd never given miscarriage much thought before. No one in my family had had one, and neither of my wife's sisters had had one either. When we found out we were pregnant with our third, I figured that our first two had gone full term and over and were born healthy—we had nothing to worry about. When my wife woke up one night and I heard screams from the bathroom, I could tell this was not normal. I can't decide which was more overwhelming, all the blood or the look on my wife's face. We rushed to the ER, hoping it was just a fluke. The entire time I was trying to remain calm and reassure my wife.

The time in the ER and following, I felt completely lost. Being a pastor and having the Bible training and

Bible knowledge, yet as a result of the miscarriage, none of the answers I was taught gave me any comfort, direction, or understanding. This was the most difficult part of the miscarriage for me, living in the reality of what happened but struggling to bridge the gap between my head knowledge and my emotions.

I also struggled supporting and comforting my wife. I found it extremely hard to comfort her when I myself was in turmoil and had absolutely no closure. To make it more difficult, my wife could remember every detail and relived it every day. I, on the other hand, dismissed many details and put all my attention on the big hurt of losing my son. Still to this day, it upsets my wife that I cannot remember the exact day we lost our son. For me, it's not the day, but the event that sticks with me.

Being the one who tried to hold it together was hard. Being a pastor, caring for others was very difficult during this time. Others worries and concerns seemed so insignificant. When there is an answer to many of their concerns, but I'm wrestling with our reality existing with no explanation, was maddening. Very few words were of any comfort to me. I can never remember a time before that I had wished I had someone else to take care of me. Losing a child made me want to put a hold on adulthood and again be a child whose parents would take care of him and handle the situation facing him. Only God's grace and power gave me the strength to persevere through this time and allowed me to heal.

Timothy's Dad

CHAPTER 10

HERE COMES ANOTHER BABY!

June 10, 2016

I can't believe it! I'm still in shock—my hopes came true! God has shown favor and mercy on us in this time of great pain, loss, and suffering. What an amazing God we serve!

I think it's a miracle that one month and one day after the miscarriage, we find out we are pregnant yet again— with our blessed fourth child! I feel so much peace, an answered prayer celebrated! And yet this sliver of fear and doubt is trying to creep in and decimate any hope, joy, or excitement we have for our baby. Can we really be prepared either way?

I'm so thankful my husband was excited too. I planted the second, positive pregnancy test where he could find it, since I'd unexpectedly found out at the doctor's office. When he found it, he gave a big smile and said, "So are you really pregnant?" with a kind, hopeful voice, waiting for the climactic answer.

I'd gone to the doctor earlier that day feeling miserable, but the only positive test was the pregnancy test! I guess

I have the nine-month sickness. It feels different this time. Instead of being a misery fest, I feel so honored and relieved to be carrying another child of ours—whom God has blessed us with, for however long or short.

God honoring Hannah with her baby Samuel, answering her prayer and desire for a child, feels like my story too (1 Samuel 1). This was also the primary scripture God led me to after losing Timothy.

That night, my husband said to me (as we were watching a terrible thunderstorm outside), "I was thinking. We have weathered many storms together and we are still together, and we are stronger for it." What a sweet thing to say! So blessed by him, God's gift to me; so glad I listened and waited for God's timing. I'm so thankful that not even this treacherous storm of losing a child could tear us apart.

Please, God, please protect our baby and let it not be harmed. In Jesus's name, *Amen.*

CHAPTER 11

MY STRUGGLE IN THE SILENT SHADOWS

August 18, 2016

Some of you may be wondering why I haven't written in so long. Well, I have been wrestling with God, avoiding Him, and so on. He has been doing undercover surgery on my heart, and today, I finally woke up.

There were three impactful trips we took this summer, all in which we were surrounded by countless godly people whom God used to wake me up. When attending the Mary & Martha Company Conference, I shared about Timothy, and I sobbed my eyes out, before I even spoke to a room full of people. But that didn't stop these women from embracing me in hugs that helped me feel so safe and so loved. One of these God-fearing women even gave me a silver, baby-feet pin that I could wear, which I'd secretly prayed for—only God knew that desire of my heart.

On another trip, a wonderful woman named Rebekah reached out to me, and we had many heart-to-heart conversations about the kind of loss(es) we had both experienced through miscarriage. She gave me such hope and comfort and the space to let me share what I have really been thinking and feeling. She could truly understand every word, from the depths of her grieved heart. I thank God for her and the specific people He has put in my life this summer to stir in me a healing that only God can perform, one only He can master.

However, the real reason I'm writing tonight is because God touched my heart through a movie called *Unconditional.* After watching this movie, I realized that through this heart-wrenching, suffocating, most agonizing grief I have ever felt in my entire being, the sun is still shining above the clouds, even when all we can see is rain, thunder, lightning, the raging winds—the storm. God's love is still there. Even through the worst storms we've ever faced, His love is still radiating, and frankly, I didn't want to believe it before now.

If God is so good, why did He let my son die? If God loves me, why did He let this happen to me? If I'm so special and haven't earned this tragedy, why me, why now, why Timothy? I still don't know any of these answers, and I don't know if I ever will. I do know there is someone out there reading this who's feeling the same way, and all I can tell you is that no matter what storm you are facing now, don't let Satan convince you it will last forever. Only God lasts forever, and God is unconditional, sacrificial love that will never let go. He hasn't left me; I have avoided Him—and God hasn't left you either.

Much more to come, about my difficult journey this summer, but also the miracles God has been working in the silence and the shadows.

CHAPTER 12

THE JOURNEY OF A COLLEGE FRIEND

August 19, 2016

This is a message I received from a college friend of mine, Phoebe, she wanted me to share her story with all of you. With her permission, this is her story:

Hey A.C. Babbitt, ,

I've been debating reaching out to you for a while now, and this morning after reading your most recent blog post God just won't let me go another day without contacting you.

I'm so sorry for what you've been going through. I remember Timothy, and I pray for you. I just wanted you to know that I'm here if you need absolutely anything. I want to support you and love you, even though I know we haven't really talked much since Moody. I can honestly say that I have a deep "understanding" of what you're going through. I obviously do not fully know your situation, and everyone is different, but the loss of a child is horrendous, and no one should have to go through that.

Earlier this year, I was officially diagnosed with "recurrent miscarriage." We've lost a total of three babies, and they are each so special and dear to me. Each time I've wrestled with God, and it has taken me time to learn from my losses and get back to the Lord. In each case, I've heard God speak. The first two times I heard Him soon after the loss. This past loss was May 29, and only recently did I realize that He spoke days later, but I was too angry to hear Him.

I'd like to tell you what I've learned. You never forget the child you lost, and you shouldn't! It's always ok to have days that are for that child—the loss date, their due date, and so on. But here has been my experience with each loss:

1) Samuel (9/29/13): After this loss I was reading the Bible, and in 1 Samuel, God calls to Samuel and tells him about the judgment that is coming for Eli and his house because of his son's sin. Samuel is terrified to tell Eli, but when Eli demands to hear what the Lord said, Samuel tells him everything, and Eli's response in 1 Samuel 3:18 is how God spoke to me: "So Samuel told him everything and hid nothing from him. And he said, 'It is the Lord. Let him do what seems good to him'" (ESV).[2]

God reminded me that He is good and that I can trust that even when my human brain can't see and understand what's going on, God is still good! At that time, I couldn't name the baby, but when I was pregnant with Joash, I was reading through 1 Samuel again, and God impressed upon my heart that the baby we lost was to be named Samuel. Just as Hannah had given her baby back to the Lord, so I had to give my Samuel back to God.

2) Achazia (2/4/16): A friend of mine and I found out we were both pregnant on the same day, and we were so excited, but within a few days, I started to lose the baby. As I was losing her, I looked up baby girl names and came across this one, Achazia. It means "God holds" and "God has taken." How fitting? As I lost her, I couldn't feel God close to me, but I *knew* that He was still holding me.

A few days later, I visited a friend who had been told she would never have kids again. During our visit, I got to hold her biological, one-month old, baby girl. Through snuggling with that little girl God reminded me that He is in control and that He knows the desires of our hearts and that, many times, in His infinite mercy, He gives us those things. She was a precious example of God fulfilling the desire of my friend's heart, and He still knows the desires of mine. [2]

---

[2] 2 "1 Samuel 3:18." The Holy Bible, English Standard Version. ESV Text Edition: 2016. Copyright © 2001 by Crossway Bibles, a publishing ministry of Good News Publishers.

3) Amana (5/29/16): This was by far my hardest loss. I wasn't expecting it. I had terrible morning sickness, and I'd been to the doctor for tests to make sure everything was going well. Then I started bleeding, I rushed to the doctor and got to see my sweet girl on the ultrasound with a heartbeat. I was so excited! They just thought the bleeding was due to some medication they had put me on to help sustain my hormones. The bleeding stopped, but then three days later, it started again. This time my visit to the doctor didn't have such good news. The gestational sac had collapsed, and my body was pushing everything out. I questioned so much—Why did you let me see my baby and her heartbeat if you were just going to take her away?

That Sunday, I couldn't stand to face the people at our church who knew we had been pregnant and then knew we had lost the baby. I couldn't do it. I couldn't handle the sympathy, the sad faces, the hugs. I just couldn't do it. So, we visited a different church in the area, and they happened to be having a testimony Sunday. The pastor's wife got up and talked about her faith struggle as they've watched their twenty-year-old son become bedridden because of Lyme disease. She was questioning God when she heard Him ask her a question back, and she finally realized God isn't done with her story yet.

That resonated so much with me, but it wasn't until a month or so later that I realized God was asking me the same thing. He wasn't done with my story yet, and because of the memory of my baby, her story isn't done yet either. She is helping others who are going through pregnancy loss, and one day I'll spend eternity with her. I couldn't name her for a very long time, but finally we settled on Amana, it's Hebrew for "faithful" because God is faithful, but that was the one thing I doubted and needed the most reminding of.

This loss is still fresh and raw for me because typically I bled for about one week after a loss and then started my next cycle. With Amana, I bled for eight weeks straight and finally thought I was done with the physical ailments of this loss. But this past Monday, I had a procedure done that verified I still have something, tissue or lining, left in that could prevent another healthy pregnancy. Through all of this, I can still hold and love on Joash, but remember that God is faithful. He isn't finished yet. He knows the desires of my heart, and will do what seems good to Him.

I hope that you can feel comfortable coming to me if you need to talk, cry, yell, pray, or whatever. I'll definitely be here for you. Feel free to call anytime. I'm praying for you and thinking about you as you go through this difficult walk. I can't take away your pain or bring

Timothy back, but I can pray for you, remember him, and speak his name.

Love,

Phoebe

* * * * *

May 31, 2019

4) Davian (11/28/16): When we found out we were pregnant; I was equal parts excited and nervous. Everything seemed to be going well, and at six weeks, we got to do the first ultrasound. The doctor couldn't see much, but just figured I might be off on how far along I thought I was, so she said to come back in two weeks, and we would see what had changed. We nervously waited, but in those two weeks, whenever I started to worry, I heard God speaking to my heart, saying, "Trust me. Just trust me," and I would be overwhelmed with the peace that surpasses understanding.

After two weeks, we went back to the doctor. I had high expectations, since we'd lost all the other babies by eight weeks, and here we were at eight weeks, and nothing bad had happened, and I'd been given God's peace repeatedly. During the ultrasound, she saw everything that would detail a healthy pregnancy, except the baby. She tried to assure us that it wasn't necessarily a bad thing. If my dates had been off, then everything could still look perfectly normal! She told us to make an appointment for another ultrasound, at the hospital, where they have better equipment, to see what was really going on. So, we started another two weeks wait, and once again, whenever I worried, God spoke to me again, "Trust me. Just trust me."

When the day came for our appointment, I was convinced that everything was going to be perfect, but when they did the ultrasound, they said that we'd had a missed miscarriage. They sent me to get blood tests done, to see if my body was realizing the loss yet, and I remember going to get the blood tests, convinced that the doctors were wrong! God had been telling me to trust Him. There was no way my baby was gone! But the blood tests showed that the doctors were right, and apparently, the baby had never grown past four to five weeks, which was why they never saw much on the ultrasounds.

To this day, I haven't had an answer from God as to why I was given such peace when everything was horribly wrong. It's been the most prominent time I've experienced God's peace. It was almost as if I couldn't worry, even if I wanted to. I may not have the answer as to why this baby died, but I do know that the peace I was given was a gift, because without it, I would've been in incredible pain and probably suffered great depression.

It took over six months for us to choose a name for this baby. I prayed and prayed about a name, but nothing was coming. We had nicknamed this baby "Baby Loved" or "Baby Beloved," because it was a baby that gave us hope for a successful pregnancy, and oh boy, was that baby loved! We finally settled on the name Davian, because it means "beloved!" It was the perfect name to go with the baby who was so deeply loved and brought us such hope.

Phoebe

CHAPTER 13

A LETTER TO MY LOST CHILD

September 21, 2016

D ear Timothy,
Oh, how I have missed you so much, my son! Though our time was short, it was a blessed chance to carry you with me for nine long weeks and six short days. I miss seeing you in heaven and hearing your voice—though am thankful God gave me the   chance, twice.

Daddy, your brother, and your sister miss you too, but I'm not   sure your brother or sister understand what happened to you. We are your family, and we will always love you—but I'm glad you have family with you up there too. Say hi to Great Grams for me and to Grandpa Lyle for Daddy, for we miss them dearly.

I can't wait to see you, but we both know I can't come yet, not until the time is right. Sometimes, I wish I could come to you now, but then I remember the only way how, and with your daddy, brother, and sister, and baby sibling on the way, I would be leaving   them behind. I can't rationalize the trade - not at this time. I hope   you are happy and safe and well loved, because I feel so helpless to be a part of making any of that happen for you.

There are so many mama things I won't get to do for you. But I hope you won't be too big for hugs, when God decides I'm ready to come where you are. I love you, son, and hope this suffering will be worth it someday.

Love,

Mom

CHAPTER 14

BATTLING THE DARKNESS OF DEPRESSION

November 14, 2016

Depression sinks the heart of the soul into the deepest, darkest, numbest, and loneliest place known to man. Your reality becomes jaded, and every part of your life darkened by the overwhelming burden of the darkness entrapment. Joy becomes indifference. Pain becomes unbearable. Simple words or acts of rejection or snark become deadly wounds inflicted with ease, stinging for a moment and then surging the darkness with yet more power over you.

Grief is an ongoing journey to find relief and acceptance of loss or rejection. And yet at this moment, I feel stuck in a pit instead of moving forward. I only move from pit to pit, depression to anger, weeping to numbness and back to depression yet again. I finally make headway and think I'm almost back to normal, but then realize normal is no longer there for me to find.

I'm changed. Losing Timothy has changed me forever. Please don't pretend I'm the same person you knew before May 2016, because I'm very much changed. No longer willing to carry burdens of failed attempts to please people and in doing so, somehow become more valuable to them. No longer can I stand petty complaints about things that won't matter much longer than they are stewed about and will pass away like grass in the fall.

Don't tell me kids aren't worth your time, sacrifice, or inconvenience. Don't tell me it's better this way. Don't tell me it's my fault for following God's timing for us to have children. If you have a problem with when I have my children, take it up with God, not me. Don't tell me you understand. Do you really understand your heart being ripped from your chest and not put back in its place? Do you understand the utter despair when your child is gone, and there is nothing in your power to save them ever?

I know God is here during my darkest despair. Though I'm numb, He takes care of me. While I'm searching for answers He won't meet, He is patient and kind. When I have lost hope, He returns it to me. Though I'm angry and hurting and want to turn from the God I thought protected me from things like this, I can't, and I won't. He is too good to me and hasn't given up on me, so why give up on Him?

Believe me: this is hard to share with all of you, but God won't let me keep it unwritten any longer. You must know this is the hardest trial I have ever faced in my life, and I've had my fair share, but God is still here with me—I just know it. All I must do is let Him pick up the pieces of my heart and add gold lacquer to mold an even more precious masterpiece than before. Father God, carry me out of this darkness and heal my innermost wounds.

Let God be God, let the healing take place, don't hold in, and don't hold back. Now it's your turn.

CHAPTER 15

THE EXPERIENCE OF A TEEN MOM

May 30, 2019

This is the testimony of a teen mom, whose desire was to help others like her, find healing. With her permission, this is her story:

When I had my miscarriage, I was in high school. I thought it was my fault. I thought this because I thought I didn't take care of myself well enough to support life. I also thought it was my fault because I wasn't married. Then I thought it was God's fault. I was really angry with Him. I distanced myself from Him for a very long time.

I finally came back to God at a conference I went to. I felt these waves of emotions coming out. I never actually cried over Sam until then. I think God made me finally realize that I could be vulnerable enough to finally mourn the death of my baby boy. I don't ever cry, and that's what I needed to do. After I cried, I wasn't angry anymore. I felt this wave of calmness. I finally forgave myself and God for what had happened to me.

This was several months after I'd lost Sam.

I have grown closer to God. I feel like he was holding my heart throughout my mourning and even after that. I'll never get over losing Sam, but it gets easier every day because I have faith that I'll see him someday. I also have God walking with me every day. I thank God for everything he has given me! He gave me a really good friend to help me through this even when I was having a hard time following him. We love you so much Sam!

Love,

Mom

CHAPTER 16

WHEN YOUR PURPOSE SEEMS LOST

November 21, 2016

When your purpose seems to be buried and you can't dig deep enough to find it, when nothing you do is working to fix it and nothing seems clear, what then?

I feel so distracted trying to find my purpose to achieve something, yet nothing is fulfilling. Nothing makes me content. I'm trying to get published as a children's author but haven't heard anything back. I'm trying to make three very part-time jobs work, but alas, I can't help but wish I was doing something else. I love my kids, and I love my husband, but I feel so overwhelmed by taking care of them all the time and not getting to work on me—my dreams, hobbies, sleep, and so on. (This is coming from taking care of two sick kids, while being sick myself, twice in three weeks, with no break in between.) Can you relate?

I feel like I should be reading Ecclesiastes or Job at this point. But where do you find your purpose? How do you stay content with the life God has given to you? How do you thank God for blessings when you are distracted by the areas you claim are lacking for you?

CHAPTER 17

THE ALMOST DUE DATE

December 6, 2016

Today was Timothy's due date. Though a very normal and pleasant day, there was still a small cloud of sadness. I'll admit I had a good cry, but I'm thankful I could cry. For so many months, I held in my grief, but that did no good. So today, I pondered our son and what could have been and wept for him, as his mommy.

It's so strange to lose one child and be pregnant with another, but I'm learning to be thankful for our fourth child being as healthy as our first. Tomorrow, I'm thirty weeks pregnant with baby number four, and it's a surreal feeling. So many women I know are due this month, in December, and I was too. I was one of them. But instead I'm now due in February.

Someday, I'll understand. Someday, I'll see why one baby needed Heaven, and the others needed me. Someday, I'll have closure and will be able to smile when I think of Timothy. Someday, I'll finally see my son face to face, no matter how old he'll be, and I'll finally be at peace, full peace indeed. Someday, I'll see why this baby's time needed to be now and why Timothy's time was so short. But today, all I know is that one baby is safe in heaven, and one is safe with me.

When people ask how I'm feeling, I'm at a loss for words. On one hand, I'm thankful for this baby God has given us after losing Timothy, but on the other, we would've taken both, given the choice. People ask how they can help, and I tell you: Please pray. Pray I can stay away from depression and stay here in reality, where my family needs me. Pray I can trust God again and learn to love Him deeper. Pray that I remember what a kind woman made very clear to me last week, "It was not your fault!" that finally broke me free from my depression.

I thank God for all of you reading this, because then our loss hasn't gone to waste. Please remember that every child counts, and every child is a blessing, no matter if we get to hold them in our arms or simply in our hearts.

CHAPTER 18

VALENTINE'S DAY

February 14, 2017

Today is Valentine's Day. We have a new member of our family to celebrate with us this year—our own little Valentine, born February 8, 2017.

She's an answer to many, many prayers to God! She was thought to be an ectopic pregnancy, and God miraculously moved her to my womb. Even though a laparoscopic surgery scope and anesthesia had the potential to have handicapping effects on her, they didn't affect her one bit. Though she was conceived shortly after the miscarriage, by God's grace, I had enough energy and support to pull through the pregnancy. Special thanks to my husband! What a trooper!

When it was known that I'm homozygous for a blood-clotting gene, and then discovered I had a bleed in my placenta—which was miraculously contained by the placenta, as a hepatoma, and taken out as three large blot clots at delivery—I praised God for protecting both her and me. I prayed not to deliver by C-section, even though with the placenta bleed, it seemed very likely. It was contained enough, and I was able to deliver vaginally, with little to-no complications.

Even through all of these answered prayers, I can't seem to let myself trust God. How do I know He won't take another child of mine? I don't. The feeling of utter helplessness and lack of control whatsoever is terrifying—and surprisingly relieving. It wasn't my fault that Timothy died. Nothing I did, said, thought, nothing, though the deceiving lie lingers to torment me away from God. I had no control over whether he lived or died, and I never have had or will have that control. I have no control over whether or not I lose my husband, my kids, or anybody for that matter. So why act like I have to be perfect in order not to lose them?

In a surprising way, this realization has freed me not to hold on to people, relationships, things, and so on with an iron grip. By no longer believing I have control and remembering God has complete control—why worry about anything when I'm powerless to change or control it? I'm not talking about not doing anything at all or not taking responsibility for my actions. That's not what I mean. I mean trusting God to take care of what you are worried about and choosing to let go of the anxious, pining-away thoughts, and move on into His freeing peace.

You don't have to fix it, because God will. You don't have to know how to figure it out, because God already has. No wonder God tells us in the book of Matthew not to worry, for it doesn't add an hour to your life (Matthew 6:25–27). In other words, it will not change anything, except make you upset, hard to talk to, and drive your spouse, your kids, and those around you away. Why, do you ask? Because who wants to be around someone who claims to know God but is so afraid?

But most of all, I prayed for her to be delivered alive and healthy, and that God wouldn't take her to Heaven yet, like he took Timothy. God kept His promises—this time. But did God really break a promise to me or relieve me of what would've been too much for me to handle?

Sometime in the last few months, during this winter, I was venting to God, alone in the basement. I kept asking God, "Why me? Why did you take Timothy? What did we do to deserve losing a child?" And for once since Timothy died, I actually stopped to listen.

God reminded me, he didn't take Timothy to punish me, but to relieve me. I couldn't have taken care of him, and He knew it would be harder for me to see him and lose him than to miscarry him. I cried and cried—finally an answer from God that gives me peace and closure.

CHAPTER 19

I DREAM OF YOU IN HEAVEN

June 3, 2019

With permission, I share this testimony is written by an anonymous mom, who was willing to share her story:

For me, my miscarriage happened very early in the pregnancy. There was nothing significant that happened that caused me to believe I'd miscarried. I went to the doctor to have an ultrasound done, the first one of the pregnancy, and it was only to make sure the child was okay and that the due date was close to what the doctors had thought. I took my mom with me because she'd never seen an ultrasound. I thought it would be neat and a meaningful moment for her to see the baby. It was during the ultrasound that the miscarriage was discovered.

I could tell something wasn't quite right as the concern grew on the technician's face as she tried to find the baby. I honestly was numb. I was feeling so bad that I'd brought my mom to this moment and feeling … feeling … the descriptor escapes me. How does one describe the feelings felt when you suddenly realize there is no longer a living child within you?

The next several days were really just a blur, and I simply went through the motions. I had to go to the hospital for a D&C procedure.

I'd mentioned that everything seemed to be just a blur, and I went from being so excited and filled with hope for the little one I carried then to complete emptiness. But there was one thing that I clung to—probably the one thing that really helped me to deal with the loss—a dream.

A pregnant woman has all kinds of dreams during pregnancy, so this dream didn't strike me as anything out of normal until I'd experienced the miscarriage. Prior to my ultrasound appointment, I'd dreamed of my grandma. She was sitting in a rocking chair, knitting what appeared to be a blanket. She told me how beautiful it was in heaven, and she looked so happy. Then she told me that this little one of mine would be cared for so much.

I wish I'd paid more attention to this dream. As with all dreams, I woke thinking, *Wow, that was quite the dream.* It wasn't until I'd lost the baby that I truly understood that dream. And I wonder why I was so blessed to have had such a dream. Knowing that God had my baby in heaven with Him gave me comfort. Between God and the dream, I was blessed to have, I made it through the days.

A very close friend gave me an angel pin with the birthstone of this child, and I'm most grateful for that pin. My baby is an angel in heaven, and someday, I'll get to meet this child.

Mom

CHAPTER 20

FEAR AMID GOD'S RESTORATION

March 17, 2017

How can I still be so afraid? How can I still doubt our God? Even after all He has done for me and all the prayers He has answered, still, a shred of terror remains.

When one or all of my three children (at home) get sick, hurt, or are away from me for more than a brief "mommy break," that shred of terror suddenly grips me and doesn't let go for a long time afterward. My husband, bless his heart and soul, tries and tries to reassure me, over and over, "Everything's fine. Everything will be *okay!*" But in that time of terror prison, I don't believe him or God—and that scares me more.

Why does the enemy still have this foothold in my life? I thought I had the closure I needed. I thought I was over the miscarriage enough to go on with my life. Was I wrong? Or is the enemy trying to keep me stuck?

This week, and a few weeks ago, for example, my sweet baby girl got a stuffy nose. Normally, this wouldn't be a big deal, except for the fact that she was two, three, and later five weeks old, at those times. When we brought her home from the hospital, and whenever we have contacted her doctor's office since then, they say, "She can't get sick until after she is six weeks old or she'll have to go to the ER," or, "Monitor her breathing to make sure she's not struggling to breath," or "Babies shouldn't run fevers before two months of age, so if she is, something is wrong."

As a parent, and as a mom who has already lost a child, how could I not be terrified that my child is in danger of dying? How could I sleep at night, knowing she could stop breathing in the middle of the night and I wouldn't know it? What if I couldn't bring her fever down? What if? What if? What if? I feel like a guinea pig running on a wheel in its cage, over and over, faster and faster - and yet, getting nowhere fast.

God is the only one who can truly calm my fears. The Bible verse that helps me the most is at the end of Psalm 139 (ESV): "Search me, O God, and know my heart. Test me and know my anxious thoughts. See if there is any offensive way in me, and lead me in the way everlasting."[3] This is my cry out to God every time I'm anxious or afraid and can't calm down on my own.

My times of feeling pure terror, also let me know God still has healing to do in my heart. Thankfully, He's not done with me yet. I'm still a broken jar of clay, but He continues to restore me with golden lacquer—into a masterpiece more beautiful than before. I must remember the gold doesn't come from me or my efforts to be perfect or try to fix the brokenness. It only comes from God; from His glory and power and majesty. That means I can't do it myself. Thankfully, that also means I'm never alone to face the brokenness.

Be confident God is always with you, and when bad things happen, know He will restore you with His golden lacquer too. [3]

---

[3] 3 "Psalm 139:23-24 (ESV) - Search me O God and." Blue Letter Bible. Accessed June 15, 2019. https://www.blueletterbible.org/esv/psa/139/23/s 617023

CHAPTER 21

THE SEARCHING DOCTOR

<u>June 16, 2019</u>

In the face of a miscarriage, sometimes doctors don't even have all the answers. With her permission, I share this doctor's story, searching for answers after her miscarriage:

I was hesitant to share my story because I felt like my loss wasn't as great as another woman's loss. Then I realized I've had the advantage of being almost ten years removed from my first miscarriage, and time has softened my experience. And I've come to realize how common pregnancy loss is, and the more we keep quiet about it, the more we make it seem like it's something to be ashamed about.

My husband and I found out I was pregnant right around our one-year wedding anniversary. We weren't really trying, but we were excited. We knew kids would be in our future. We just didn't think it would be so soon. Once we hit the eight-week mark, we decided to tell our parents because we were so excited to announce the first grandchild on either side of the family. Within a week of telling everyone, I started to get some cramping and bleeding. I knew something was wrong, and after a week or two of declining hCG levels, we had to call our family back and tell them the news.

At the time, it was heartbreaking of course. Because of my medical background, I kept trying to search for answers. Was it the vigorous exercise routine I'd been keeping up? Was it the tour of the manufacturing plant that I had taken a week ago that was leeching fumes into the air? I wanted to blame it on something. While going through the experience of my miscarriage, I uncovered many miscarriages in my family and learned more about the MTHFR mutation. I decided to get tested and found I did have one of the mutations. After finding out, I did change my diet a little and changed my prenatal vitamin and some other supplements. Within a couple months, I found out I was pregnant again and went on to have a healthy pregnancy and baby.

After another miscarriage and another healthy pregnancy and baby, and having heard many stories of loss, I know now that the miscarriages didn't happen because of something I did, or because of some genetic mutation. Through the years, my faith has grown stronger, and I believe there is an ultimate plan for me. Even though I don't always totally understand, it gives me comfort to know God loves us and He is directing our path.

Doctor Mom

CHAPTER 22

EASTER REFLECTIONS

April 26, 2017

I have been pondering this since Easter Sunday, about two weeks now, and to be honest, avoiding it as well. I must admit I can't stop thinking about last year at this time and how unaware I was of what was about to happen.

A year ago, Easter Sunday, I remember not fitting well into the dress I'd put on to wear to church that morning. I remember thinking how odd that was and just shrugged it off as bloating and wore it anyway. After church, when we got home, we took our own family photo, since we were all dressed up and smiley. Little did I know that day, I was already pregnant with Timothy, and that would be our only family picture with him in it—ever.

It's funny how fast a year can pass, and I have never been more thankful that this one has. Yet there is a part of me deeply missing those few, short weeks in which my precious baby Timothy was with me. I wish I'd been more grateful at the time he was in my womb. That he was growing for the first month of life in the womb. I wish I knew the exact day he died so I could mourn and remember him on that day. Instead, I mourn him on the day my body fully miscarried him, the worst day I could ever imagine. Yet I remember that day being filled with the strongest peace I've ever felt.

I still don't understand how God would willingly give up His son to die for ungrateful humanity, who continually mess up and treat God as if He doesn't exist or isn't worthy of everything and more. He chose to give Jesus up to die, but I know I wouldn't have made the same choice. I can't even put into words how much I miss my son and how devastated and grieved my heart is, aching for just a touch or a sound or a glimpse of him.

I can feel my hard heart toward God getting worse as the anniversary of his death, May 9, 2016, draws near. I can't even bring myself to talk about it anymore, like my heart is shut away in a locked vault no one can open. I keep waiting for the day I'll feel normal again, when I can stop worrying about my other children's safety, to the point of utter panic, because I can't bear the thought of losing another child. I'm driving my husband crazy because I can't relax and let up a bit when it comes to games or activities that have even the slightest potential to hurt them or him. I'm not the same person and I'm afraid I'll never be normal again.

Although I have been avoiding time with God, I forced myself to listen to the audio Bible app we have and felt led to listen to the books of James and 1 Peter. I'm still amazed at how relevant the Bible is, no matter what I'm going through. James was a great reminder of how destructive sin can be, and no matter how I feel, there's no excuse for sin. First Peter talked about persevering through suffering and how Christ is our example to follow in that suffering. Suffering because of sin or bad choices means nothing, but suffering humbly for Christ is of great value and is precious in His sight. There was more to it, but that's what stuck out to me.

I don't have a magic answer for anyone who is suffering out there, but I do know God is the only one who can truly comfort and heal you. Pray to Him and let Him try. What else do you have to lose? We are in this together, and together God's family remains.

Jesus, save a spot for me, at the marriage supper of the lamb, right next to my son. We will have a lot to catch up on.

Love,

A.C. Babbitt

CHAPTER 23

IN THE MEANTIME

September 18, 2017

I'm surprised to find myself here again, writing to all of you. Yet, here I am. I find myself struggling again. Yet again I wrestle with the reality that my child is gone. I didn't expect to still be struggling. I thought I was fine. I thought I'd moved past his death. I thought having a baby after him would fix it too, but she didn't. Don't get me wrong. She's a joy and blessing all her own, but he's still gone.

For some reason, the grief and anger and bitterness toward God are coming back in strong waves, trying to knock me over. A year ago, it made sense to be struggling, but now, I don't quite understand why.

My oldest, our now three-year-old son, keeps bringing up Timothy, his little brother, and I'm not sure why he has been so often lately. Today, he said that when we get to heaven, his baby sister and Timothy can play together, and he can run in between them. Although I appreciate his imagination and caring heart, it makes me sad. Oh, how long it will be before all my sweet children will be together in heaven—if they all know Jesus, that is.

Even our two-year-old daughter has begun talking about her little brother. I'm beginning to wonder if they know something I don't, if there's some way God is revealing him to them that I don't know about. Even in public, she'll start talking about him, and people get confused, and correct her, thinking she's talking about her baby sister. Oh, how my heart hurts and longs for my lost baby boy, my son.

Can anyone relate to my struggles? It has been almost a year and a half, and there are still times I grieve losing my son. Yesterday, we had our youngest girl dedicated at church. During the dedication, it hit me—we'd be dedicating Timothy instead of her right now. We'll never dedicate him here because he's already with God. We'll never hold him in our arms and show him to our family who came to watch, because he isn't here.

My oldest keeps reminding me how he wishes Timothy was here, that he would come here, that he would come back. Oh, how the tears come in those moments. Even my sweet three-year-old knows the loss of his brother and misses him. But you know what? He also reminds me to have hope, that this life isn't forever, and life with God, and with Timothy, is. When that day comes, I know I'll see my son, and when I do, I'll hug him and say, "I love you, son. I've missed you so!"

I have to be honest I have been struggling to bring my struggles to God. Even though I know He's the only one who can fix my pain, heal my hurt, I still resist. Although we are beyond blessed by our baby girl and other children, why couldn't we have him too? I don't know if I'll ever understand God's plan, but what I do know is that God does not withhold good from those who walk uprightly (Psalm 84:11 ESV), and He is always with me (Deuteronomy 31:6 ESV). He holds every tear in His hand, and I hope for the day when He will wipe away every tear from every eye (Isaiah 25:8; Revelation 21:4 ESV), of every mom and dad who have lost precious children they love more than life itself. And that day, when we see our babies again, will be the most glorious day in eternity—and that day is worth waiting for!

CHAPTER 24

THE TESTIMONY OF A TEEN FATHER

May 30, 2019

This is a teen dad, dealing with the grief and anger because of the miscarriage, and his journey to find peace. With his permission, this is his story: When the mother of my son and I found out that we'd lost him, we were devastated. At first, I didn't know what to think. We were both in high school and seemed to be too young to have to deal with such a thing as this. I felt completely lost and alone. I felt angry toward almost everything for a short while, because of my lack of knowledge about what I should do.

I was furious at God for allowing such a thing to happen to my son, and then I was furious at myself, feeling as if I'd failed as a father. This cycle of anger and grief continued until I did something that I feel I should have done from the very beginning. I read my Bible and looked up verses that helped bring me peace after getting some much-needed advice and support from my youth pastors during high school.One of these verses that I found to be extremely helpful in this time was Jeremiah

1:5: "Before I formed you in the womb I knew you, before you were born I set you apart; I appointed you as a prophet to the nations" (NIV). This verse helped me know that God had a plan for me and my son, Sam, before Sam was even conceived. After I'd the much-needed counseling, I finally felt a strange feeling that I haven't felt for a long time, not since before we discovered we lost Sam. By the grace of God, I finally felt peace.

Overall, what I discovered is that even during what seems to be the lowest point of your life, you're never too far from the grace of God and the healing power He can extend.

Dad

CHAPTER 25

FIGHTING BITTERNESS AND EXPECTATIONS

November 12, 2017

Six years ago, today, my husband proposed to me. Six years ago, today, I had such high hopes for my life, our to-be marriage, our future kids, so on and so forth. I had certain expectations of what our future might hold or what I thought it should hold for us, down the road. I never thought we would lose a baby. I never expected it would happen to us. Now things look a lot different than I expected—but not a bad, terrible, unbearable different. A good, not always easy, but definitely not what I'd hoped, different.

The past few months have been a struggle. I've been feeling so angry toward God, blaming Him for taking Timothy away from me. Why didn't He protect him? Why did He let my baby die? However, this anger and blame has turned into a deep pit of bitterness and rebellion toward God. I have been purposely avoiding spending time with God. I know I should read my Bible, but I have little to no desire to read it.

My heart is hard, and it aches, but I think the bitterness has done more damage than the grief. My temper tantrum is getting old, and I know it. Turning my back on God doesn't give me the control over my life I wish I had to bring my son back.

I asked a friend today who has also lost babies, "How do you stop blaming or being mad at God?"And she replied, "Is it really His fault? Did He cause it? Why isn't it Satan's fault? Why is it anyone's fault? Don't you think God is big enough to handle your anger? If you want to be mad, be mad and pour it out to Him. But don't let it make you bitter. Being mad and blaming God can lead to bitterness. God can handle your anger, but you can't keep holding on to it, or it will make you bitter. Cast *all* your cares on Him for He cares for you!"

She also reminded me, "God doesn't always give us what we want, but He gives us what we need." This is easier to see now than it was before, now that our baby girl is nine months old. I got pregnant with her one week after we lost Timothy, and she is a miracle and joy to behold. She has such a contagious smile and giggle, I can't imagine life without this sweet, little girl of ours. But God knew we needed her at this time, and His timing is perfect. My two older children don't always get along with each other, but they adore their little sister, and they each have their own special relationships with her. I wouldn't trade her for anything or anyone, even though I still wish I had Timothy too.

As the same friend put it, "Focus on the little blessings you do   have. God is taking care of Timothy. And Timothy won't know the sadness and sin of this world, He gets God and will only know perfect joy. Your glass is half full. Remember that." Bit by bit, God is breaking through to my hardened heart, and I have hope that the struggle will not last forever.

I pray for those of you out there who have lost babies, and some   who I know have very recently. God isn't punishing you—He is holding you and your baby/babies in His hands. He didn't take them away from us. He is saving them for us in heaven, where we will be with them again. And what a great day of rejoicing in heaven that will be!

May God give you the peace, comfort, and reassurance you   need today, to heal and encourage others to do the same. May you not be overcome with bitterness, but may God help you to grieve and move forward. *Amen.*

CHAPTER 26

GOD'S FAITHFULNESS

May 9, 2018

Two years ago today, we lost our precious Timothy Lyle Babbitt to miscarriage at nine weeks and six days. To tell you the truth, I never thought I would see a day that would be joyful ever again— but I was wrong. The last two years have been a deep struggle, and we endured much heartache, but the last two years have also brought us much love, faith, and joy we didn't expect.

One week after we lost Timothy, we got pregnant with our fourth child. She was born in February of last year, and is fifteen months old, as of yesterday. She is one of God's most precious gifts to us, and one I'm amazed by every day. A beautiful blend of adventure and intense love (meaning intense hugs and kisses, along with snuggles when you least expect it). I'm so blessed by her and the timing with which God brought her to us. I'd be lying if I told you it was easy to carry one baby while missing another, and I don't pretend to understand God's plan going this way, but I'm so glad she's ours too.

What most of you don't know is that we are now expecting baby number five as well, another baby girl! God doesn't just add to our lives; in many ways He multiplies. He has multiplied our children beyond our understanding and has blessed us beyond belief. I'm in such awe that God has chosen to give us so many babies when I know many women who don't get the chance. I promise I don't take that for granted, and to be honest, each of our babies is a miracle in his or her own way.

When people find out how many children we have, they say things like "Wow!" and "You've got your hands full!" and "No, you don't look old enough to have that many children," and "You had them really close together!" I don't know about other moms out there with more than two children, but these sayings get really old really quick, so if you are one of those people who says these things, please find something more encouraging to say that builds up these blessed mamas and doesn't make them feel ashamed of the children God has blessed them with. Especially when you don't know if they have lost babies/children along the way, please be mindful of what you say.

What I really want to tell you is that the day our baby died was not the end. It was only part of our family journey. There's life after death, and there's joy after the mourning. I'm so blessed to know Jesus has my baby right now, safe and sound, and how I experienced my baby's death isn't the end of his story and not the end of mine. Today was a sad day, but not all of it—we experienced so much joy today and so much love. While today we remember as Timothy's birthday, we also remember God's faithfulness in giving life and life abundantly, and giving hope of life after death, eternal life in Jesus Christ, our Lord and Savior. I wouldn't be here today without Jesus in my life, because He has saved my life, many times, and I pray you find Him too.

CHAPTER 27

A STORY OF UNPLEASANT SURPRISE

<u>May 23, 2019</u>

This story is told by a friend of mine, who had to experience the loss of her child, as well as the loss of her dad, in the same year. With her permission, this is her story:

In January of 2012, we were surprised to find out that we were pregnant. It was not planned, and it came as a great shock to us. But only eight weeks later, we found out that bundle of joy we had gotten so excited about was no longer going to be ours. I suffered a miscarriage, and so I began the grief of losing a baby.

I felt so alone. None of my friends had talked about miscarriages. There was such a stigma to stay quiet and not talk about it, so I didn't know who to turn to. Kyle and I prayed that we would someday be blessed with a healthy child, and we accepted that this baby was just not meant to be.

In March of 2012, our family doctor found a large mass on my dad's brain but reassured us that he thought it looked benign. But he wanted further testing done. My dad was scheduled for brain surgery that next morning to dissect what had been found.

After the surgery, a few hours later, finally the surgeon entered the room. He had a very somber look on his face, and we all knew. The surgeon went on to tell our family that he had found the mass on Dad's brain to be a stage four glioblastoma brain tumor. The life expectancy for this type of cancer was at most a few years. I immediately became sick and ran to the nearest bathroom. After gathering myself, I returned to the family room to find my mom in a pool of tears, and my brother and husband trying to make sense of what had just been shared with us.

That night, none of us got any sleep. I remember thinking, *Why God? Why us, why Dad, why me? What have we done to deserve this?* I knew at this point that this was out of my hands, and I needed to turn to prayer. I grabbed my mom's hands and embraced her in that hotel bathroom and just prayed. Prayed that it wasn't true, prayed that Dad could overcome this, prayed for strength that we would need to get through this difficult time.

Thinking back to the miscarriage I'd had a few months prior; I knew God had a plan. He knew I couldn't handle the stress of Dad's diagnosis and being pregnant at the same time.

In August, we found out we were, once again, pregnant. I didn't know how I'd be able to have a healthy pregnancy while going through this cancer journey with my dad. I was so full of fear and sadness, that I was almost positive this pregnancy would end up in a miscarriage too. I knew all

I could do was pray and trust in God's timing. When in a fearful situation, fear can overcome our faith. But I knew I needed to remain faithful, place my faith in Jesus, and believe He had it under control.

The year went on, and Dad continued treatments, but wasn't getting any better. I began to lose hope, lose faith in God, and I thought I'd take it in my own hands, because God was doing nothing. He wasn't listening to our pleading prayers; He didn't give me any "signs." He sure didn't have this under control.

Our biggest danger as Christians, is not believing God has it under control. Mark 4:39-41 states,

He got up, rebuked the wind and said to the waves, "Quiet! Be still!" Then the wind died down and it was completely calm. He said to his disciples, "Why are you so afraid? Do you still have no faith?" They were terrified and asked each other, "Who is this? Even the wind and the waves obey him!" (Mar 4:39–41 NIV)44

---

[4] "Mark 4:39 (NIV) - He got up rebuked the." Blue Letter Bible. Accessed Jun 15, 2019. https://www.blueletterbible.org/niv/mar/4/39/s_ 961039.

To me, that meant, "Quiet, be still and listen to the voice of God." I felt that I'd tried but was not getting an immediate response. Therefore, it turned me off from prayer. God was showing His authority and control over our lives. My biggest mistake was believing I could do this on my own and that I was in control. I quickly learned that that wasn't possible.

On March 10, 2013, one year and two days after the dreadful diagnosis, God blessed us with a healthy baby girl. Lauren brought a lot of joy into our lives during such a sorrowful time.

On April 16, 2013, just five weeks after having Lauren, my dad took his last breath, surrounded by his family. He had fought the good fight, and his time on earth was complete.

After losing Dad, I became mad, mad at God, mad at the doctors. I really was just not a happy person. I was supposed to be this new mom, so full of joy and happiness. I was just blessed with a beautiful baby, and all I could do was get lost in the grief of losing my dad. I became so angry when people would tell me God has a plan. I'd prayed for answers and felt no answers were given, and I continually asked why.

I began to spiral downward. I didn't go to church, didn't read the Bible, didn't pray anymore. The moment I knew I needed some serious help was when I was sitting in traffic with my two-month-old, daughter in the back seat and wanted to just pull out and end it all there. Grief had consumed me, far more than I could take. After getting home, Kyle and I sat down and discussed what I needed to do.

Without afflictions in our lives, we may never grow in our faith. We must learn to rely on the strength of God when we have weaknesses or turmoil in our lives, for only God knows our plan.

Philippians 4:6–7 (NIV) says, "Do not be anxious about anything, but in every situation, by prayer and petition, with thanksgiving, present your requests to God. And the peace of God, which transcends all understanding, will guard your hearts and your minds in Christ Jesus."[55] I continued to pray that God would show me the way to happiness.

Looking back, I know it was Him that gave us Lauren, which was happiness in such a sorrowful time. It was him that placed us in Cedar Falls, where I met the friends and mentors, I needed to get over this severe grief. He knew the plan all along. Just as Jeremiah 29:11–13 (NIV) says,

---

[5] "Philippians 4:6–7 (NIV) - Do not be anxious about." Blue Letter Bible. Accessed June 15, 2019. https://www.blueletterbible.org/niv/phl/4/6/s_ 1107006.
[6] "Jeremiah 29:11–13 (NIV) - For I know the plans." Blue Letter Bible. Accessed June 15, 2019. https://www.blueletterbible.org/niv/jer/29/11s 774011.

"'For I know the plans I have for you,' declares the Lord, 'plans to prosper you and not to harm you, plans to give you hope and a future. Then you will call on me and come and pray to me, and I will listen to you. You will seek me and find me when you seek me with all your heart.'"66

As promised, the Heavenly Father has truly become my ever-present parent, never forsaking, always uplifting, always guiding. Always there. We are not left alone in our grief. "The Lord is close to the brokenhearted and saves those who are crushed in spirit" (Psalm 34:18 NIV).67

My continued prayer for myself is that I'll find comfort through my faith and find a tangible task to approach the emptiness that was caused through losing my dad. I'm trying to complete things my dad didn't finish on earth, I continue traditions I had with him, and I keep him present in my daily life. But most of all, I try to find comfort in knowing that Dad is with our Heavenly Father and that someday I'll join them for eternity.

Jamay P.

---

6 "Psalm 34:18 (NIV) - The Lord is close to." Blue Letter Bible. Accessed June 15, 2019. https://www.blueletterbible.org/niv/psa/34/18/s 512018.

CHAPTER 28

FOR NEWLY GRIEVED MOMS AND DADS

July 22, 2018

This post is dedicated to those moms and dads who have recently, or at any time, lost a precious baby, under any circumstance, at any time during or after pregnancy.

What I'm about to say is heavy on my heart. In the last two months, I've known at least three women who have lost babies. Every time I hear of someone else losing a baby, I can't help but grieve with them, with a heavy heart, wanting so badly to hug them and give them any comfort I can. There really isn't much to say in that moment— even having gone through it myself—I'm hyperaware of how hurtful what others say can be in that moment.

But what I really want to do is share with them the freeing truths I have learned along the way, these last two years, and I hope these encourage others of you as well:

1. ***It's not your fault!*** If you could have done anything in your power to prevent it, with the full knowledge of

what was going on (which we usually don't have), you would've done it. Also, take others' ignorant and insensitive words with a grain of salt. They're just trying to help, even when it doesn't. Don't let those words plague your thoughts and make you feel badly.

2. ***You are still an amazing Mom/Dad!*** Losing a child is not a failure and does not lessen your value as a parent at all!

3. ***Though God is in control, He did not create death.*** God is still a loving God who loves your baby more than you do and hasn't forsaken you or your baby. Though there are many reasons babies don't survive, God is taking care of each and every one of them—and I know I'm so excited to see my Timothy in heaven someday! This, for me, is the hardest to wrestle with but the most important to understand and soak in.

4. ***Though it's the worst pain I've ever felt, God still has a plan.*** Since the miscarriage, I have met countless women who have miscarried, had stillborn babies, or lost babies shortly after they were born. I can't tell you how many times God helped me share their pain, because I'd experienced it too. Not only that, but also losing one baby helped me value my children at home that much more. As a mom, it's so easy to get overwhelmed and distance yourself from your family

at times. The miscarriage helped me clearly see the true value of a child—that not all are blessed with and not all get to keep.

5. ***Don't let the fear of losing another child keep you from trying to have more children.*** Don't let the enemy steal your joy and steal life from your family. Currently, I'm on my fifth pregnancy (second since the miscarriage), and I long for the innocence I had with my first two pregnancies, that pure trust that everything would turn out all right, and that we would most certainly bring our baby home. But God is not a God of fear, but of restoration and redemption. He chose to give up His only Son, Jesus, so that we may live. I know I couldn't make that choice but am glad I don't have to.

6. ***You are not alone in your loss or grief.*** So many women around the world have lost babies. Don't let yourself stay in this dark, overwhelming, suffocating, grief alone. Find someone you trust and let them listen and help you through this time. We can't overcome and heal on our own. We need the love and support of others to get us through, and speak truth into our lives, but most of all, we need God's help, the ultimate healer. Also, husbands grieve too, just differently. Don't expect them to grieve like you, but don't negate

their grief either. They may just be hiding it, so you don't feel worse.

7. ***Killing or harming yourself will not fix anything or ease the pain.*** This may seem extreme to include, but I know I felt like this during my grief process, and I'm so thankful I got help and didn't stay silent—please tell someone or simply go to the ER/your doctor if you are feeling this way—don't go through with your harmful plan and you don't have to feel this way forever, it will get better. I promise!

In my heart of hearts, I hope this is encouraging and helpful to at least one mom or dad out there, struggling with the grief of a precious little one. You are not alone, and the pain will lessen, but you never forget them. Please know you are loved, you are prayed for, and you will heal.

Sending much Love, Hugs, and Blessings,
A.C. Babbitt
Timothy's Mom

CHAPTER 29

GOD IS OPENING NEW DOORS

May 23, 2019

G od has been nudging me for a while to write this book, three years actually, since we lost our son, Timothy. According to God, He thinks I'm finally ready to write this book, and I hope I'm up to the task.

I kid you not. It was three years to the day we lost him that I got a call from a man, with the title literary agent, of a publishing house! I've been praying for a long time to find a publisher, to know how to publish a book, and to find a literary agent. Why, I even asked my husband just that morning, "How do I even find a literary agent?" God is so good, beyond all we could ask or think, and loves us fiercely. Don't forget that!

To those moms and dads who have lost children, you're not alone. There are so many of us who share your pain. God has not forgotten you, your spouse, or your child. He knows. Pursue His love, peace, and comfort. You'll never be the same, but you'll be better for it. May there be more joy than sorrow, more laughing than crying, more love than bitterness, and more hope than despair.

You are loved. You are precious. You are His child. May you be beyond blessed in the years to come. In Jesus's name, Amen.

God Bless,

A.C. Babbitt

Timothy's Mom

P.S. In the end, I chose a different publishing house, but am thankful for the reassurance of God's timing and guidance.

ABOUT THE AUTHOR

A.C. Babbitt is a Christian author, blogger, proofreader and mentor to other aspiring authors. She released her debut book, "The Miscarriage Project", 2019, and her new children's book series, "Princess with a Purpose", 2021, with book one, "Princess Amora" (#1 New Release in 4 Amazon Categories, Nov. 2021).

Babbitt also runs her own Christian lifestyle blog, entitled The Haven. She regularly writes about the Bible, her faith, and living BOLD (Beautiful-Overcomer-Loved-Designed).

She has been featured on CBN (Christian Broadcasting Network, Nov. 2020). She attended Moody Bible Institute, studying Children's Ministry, and graduated with a B.S. in Biblical Studies, with high honors.

She is currently working on several new books. These include two children's books, "My Brother in Heaven" and the second book in the "Princess with a Purpose" series. Babbitt is finishing her first YA novel titled, "The Haven Diaries Series #1: Dating, Purity and the Unknown".

She has served in youth ministry with her husband for over 12 years. They've been married for nine years and have six children. She enjoys living in the Midwest, USA. Babbitt believes when you understand and apply God's Word to your life, you and your family can thrive!

Website: acbabbitt.com
Facebook: @acbabbittauthor
Instagram: @acbabbittauthor

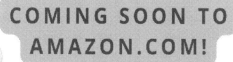

Notes

Made in the USA
Monee, IL
13 October 2022